Amazing Nature

Clever Camouflage

John Woodward

Heinemann
LIBRARY

www.heinemann.co.uk/library
Visit our website to find out more information about **Heinemann Library** books.

To order:
 Phone 44 (0) 1865 888066
 Send a fax to 44 (0) 1865 314091
Visit the Heinemann Bookshop at www.heinemann.co.uk/library to browse our catalogue and order online.

First published in Great Britain by Heinemann Library, Halley Court, Jordan Hill, Oxford OX2 8EJ, part of Harcourt Education. Heinemann is a registered trademark of Harcourt Education Ltd.

Produced for Heinemann Library by Discovery Books Limited.

Editorial: Jilly Attwood, Kate Bellamy and Helen Dwyer
Design: David Poole and Barry Dwyer
Picture Research: Rachel Tisdale
Production: Séverine Ribierre

Originated by Ambassador Litho Ltd
Printed in China by South China Printing Company

ISBN 0 431 18569 7
08 07 06 05 04
10 9 8 7 6 5 4 3 2 1

British Library Cataloguing in Publication Data
Woodward, John
Clever Camouflage - (Amazing Nature)
578.4'7
A full catalogue record for this book is available from the British Library.

Acknowledgements
The publishers would like to thank the following for permission to reproduce photographs: Bruce Coleman Collection pp. **7** (Kim Taylor), **14** (Stephen J Krasemann), **16** (Gunter Ziesler), **20** & **21** (Joe McDonald), **24** (Kim Taylor), **25** (M P L Fogden); Corbis p. **26**; FLPA pp. **6** & **9** (Jurgen & Christine Sohns). **13br** (Colin Marshall), **15r** (B Borrell Casals), **28** (G Van Frankenhuysen/ Dembinsky); Natural History Photographic Agency pp. **4** & **10** (James Carmichael jr), **11b** (Daniel Heuclin), **12** (Ant Photo Library), **13tl** (Trevor McDonald), **15l** (B Jones & M Shimlak), **18** (Norbert Wu), **22** (James Carmichael jr); Oxford Scientific Films pp. **5** (Michael Fogden), **8** (Peter Cook), **11t** (Alastair Shay), **17** (Daniel Wills/SAL), **19** (Max Gibbs), **23**, **29** (Deni Brown); Photodisc p. **27**

Cover photograph of a leaf-tailed gecko by Jurgen & Christine Sohns, reproduced with permission of FLPA.

Every effort has been made to contact copyright holders of any material reproduced in this book. Any omissions will be rectified in subsequent printings if notice is given to the publishers.

Contents

Any words appearing in the text in bold, **like this**, are explained in the Glossary.

Disguise and survival

Camouflage is all about pretending to be something you are not. We often connect it with soldiers and military vehicles, carefully coloured to match the landscape so that they are hard to see. Animals, however, have been using this type of camouflage for millions of years.

Animals have two good reasons for being well camouflaged. Many risk being killed and eaten by other animals, so making themselves harder to see helps them to survive. Killers also benefit from camouflage. It makes them less likely to be recognized by their **prey** — until it is too late.

This cricket's amazing camouflage makes it almost invisible among the moss of a Costa Rican rainforest.

The cryptic coloration of the Asian horned frog makes it look just like a dead leaf lying on the forest floor.

Types of camouflage

There are two main types of camouflage. The most common is called **cryptic coloration**. This is when animals have a pattern of colours that matches their surroundings, and makes their own shape less obvious.

The other type of camouflage is called **mimicry**. The animal has a pattern and shape that make it look like something quite different. If it wants to scare away enemies, it might look like an animal with a nasty bite or sting. But some hunters mimic harmless animals, or even plants, so they can fool their victims into thinking they are safe.

The most amazing camouflage is a mixture of cryptic coloration and mimicry. The **disguise** is so perfect that you could be looking straight at the animal, yet not know it was there.

Natural deception

Animals with clever **camouflage** have gained it gradually, through a process called **natural selection**. It works like this. Imagine a lot of mice feeding among dead brown leaves in a wood. All of the mice are different colours of yellow, grey and brown, just as people have hair of different colours. If a mouse-eating hawk flies overhead, it will see some of the mice more easily than others, and eat them first. The mice that are most likely to escape will be the brown ones, because they accidentally match their background.

When the surviving mice **breed**, they tend to pass on their colour to their young. Since the brown mice are more likely to survive and breed than the yellow or grey ones, most of the young mice will be brown. If the mice continue to eat among brown leaves for long enough, the group of mice will nearly all be brown.

Small animals like wood mice are eaten by all kinds of hunters. Mice that are harder to see are more likely to survive and breed.

Changing moths

The peppered moth is proof that natural selection works. Peppered moths normally have pale, speckled wings that make them hard to see when they sit on tree trunks. However there is also a dark form of peppered moth that is easier to see. Birds usually kill and eat more of the dark sort, so it is quite rare.

A century ago, however, the bark of trees in smoky, **industrial** towns turned very dark. This made the dark moths harder to see, so more survived. It also meant that the pale moths became easier to see on the dark bark, and more were killed. So over time, peppered moths in smoky towns were more likely to be dark.

The normal pale form of the peppered moth (right) has the best camouflage here, but the dark form is harder to spot on dark tree bark in smoky towns.

Blending with bark

Many animals live or rest on tree trunks and branches. They could make easy targets for birds and other animals that hunt by sight in the trees. So over time, some have developed amazingly good **camouflage** that makes them hard to see. They include a group of birds called the nightjars and frogmouths, which hunt by night and **roost** on branches during the day. A nightjar's **plumage** matches the tree bark almost perfectly, and it always squats down so its body looks like part of the branch. It also closes its big eyes, so they do not give it away by reflecting a glint of sunshine.

Some of these birds have another trick. The Australian tawny frogmouth perches along a big branch, rather than across it, and if it is alarmed it 'freezes' with its eyes shut and its head pointing up at an angle. In this position it looks just like the broken end of a smaller branch that has snapped off.

The bristly feathers around the bill of the tawny frogmouth look just like the torn bark of a broken branch.

Can you see the front leg of this leaf-tailed gecko? And have you noticed that there are two geckos in the picture?

Flaky lizards

Many of the climbing lizards called geckos are camouflaged so they are hard to see on trees. One of the best **disguises** belongs to the common leaf-tailed gecko, which lives on the island of Madagascar. This gecko's skin looks just like flaking bark. It even has a fringe of small, ragged flaps of skin that blend with the tree's bark. The flaps mask the gecko's shape, and also cover up its shadow.

Thorns, twigs and leaves

The real masters of **disguise** are various types of insects. Thanks to their hard, plastic-like skin, the bodies of insects can be formed into all sorts of strange shapes. Many insects don't look like animals at all. They are plant mimics.

Some sit on plants and suck their sugary **sap**. They are easy targets for insect-eaters, so they try to stay out of trouble by looking like part of the plant. Many look almost exactly like thorns growing on the plant stem, and others resemble buds or flowers.

The hard, spiny bodies of these **tropical** thorn bugs look and even feel like bits of the plant that they feed on.

The most famous plant mimics are the stick insects that some people keep as pets. Their bodies are stretched out so they look like twigs, and many have knobs and spines that are just like those of plants. A few even have extra decorations that look like the tufts of moss that often grow on twigs.

The closely related leaf insects are even more amazing. They have flattened bodies that are almost exactly like leaves, complete with leaf-like **veins**, **midribs** and stalks. Even their legs have flattened extensions so they look like small leaves. Many leaf insects are green, but others are brown, like dead leaves. Some even have ragged edges so they seem to have been chewed by leaf-eating caterpillars.

Looking exactly like a slightly withered, nibbled leaf, the amazing leaf insect is one of the finest plant mimics.

Gecko and leaf insect links

One of the leaf-tailed geckos that lives on Madagascar has the same type of **camouflage** as a leaf insect. Its brown body and tail are twisted so they look like a dead leaf drying out in the sun.

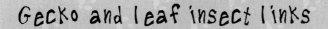

If you were a lizard hunter you would have a hard job finding this leaf-tailed gecko.

11

Seaweed surprise

The seaweedy decorations of a leafy sea dragon make a perfect disguise in the weedy shallows of the Australian coral seas.

It's not just land animals that pretend to be plants. Many sea creatures have **camouflage** that makes them look just like bits of seaweed. One example is the leafy sea dragon, which is a type of seahorse. It lives in shallow seawater off the coasts of southern Australia. Its body is covered with long, leafy flaps that look exactly like **fronds** of seaweed. As it hangs around among the real seaweed, sucking in tiny animals from the water, its leafy fronds sway about just like the real thing.

A fish from the Atlantic Ocean uses the same trick. It's called the sargassum fish, because it lives among the seaweed that floats near the surface of the Sargasso Sea near Bermuda. The sargassum fish uses its strange hand-like front fins to crawl about among the weed, and is almost impossible to see because of its 'seaweedy' **disguise**.

Twigs and spines

The scorpion fish that live among rocks in shallow water have camouflage that makes them look like rocks encrusted with sea life. Their skins are covered with leafy or twig-like growths that look like seaweeds, corals and marine (sea) worms.

Scorpion fish and crab links

Unlike scorpion fish, decorator crabs do not grow disguises on their skin but they do deliberately plant seaweed and animals on their shells, attaching them to special hooked hairs. They cover themselves up so well that their true shape is almost invisible.

The coloured lumps on the skin of this scorpion fish are a perfect match with the sea life on the rocks.

This decorator crab is completely concealed beneath the discs of purple coral that it has planted on its back.

mimicry and bluff

Most **camouflaged** animals depend on looking like their surroundings, but some have a different tactic. They try to look like something that is nasty to eat, or even something dangerous.

The young caterpillars of swallowtail butterflies have slimy-looking greenish-black and white skin that makes them look like bird droppings. Many caterpillars are eaten by birds, but since birds normally avoid eating their own droppings, the caterpillars are safe, even though they are easy to see against the green leaves.

Other caterpillars change their shape, and pretend to be dangerous snakes. The elephant hawkmoth caterpillar has a spot on each side of its body, just behind its small head. If it is scared it pulls its head back into its body, and this makes the spots bulge out so they look like big eyes. Any bird that tries to eat it is likely to get a fright, and fly off.

A harmless caterpillar from Costa Rica scares away its enemies by pretending to be a deadly viper.

Striped mimics

Some insects mimic wasps with painful stings. This is easy to do, because wasps have a warning pattern of yellow and black that is easily recognized by other animals, including humans. A variety of flies and moths have the same colour scheme, and it probably helps protect them from birds that normally avoid attacking wasps. These mimics include the hoverflies that gather **nectar** from garden flowers, and the harmless but scary-looking hornet clearwing moth.

Insect and octopus links

While an insect will mimic only one type of animal, the amazing Indonesian mimic octopus can pretend to be all kinds of dangerous animals. It can crawl across the sea floor like a crab, swim like a jellyfish, or pretend to be a deadly poisonous sea snake.

Yellow and black stripes usually mean trouble, but this hoverfly is harmless. It just wants to be left alone.

The mimic octopus can change its shape to resemble quite different animals, including some that could kill you.

Quick-change artists

The most startling **camouflage** tactic is the ability to change colour, pattern and shape, within a few minutes or even seconds. Some lizards called chameleons are famous for this. A chameleon's skin is covered with tiny dots of different colours. Each dot can be made bigger, or it can be squeezed so small that it is invisible. So if the chameleon squeezes all its yellow dots shut and opens the red dots wide, it changes colour from yellow to red.

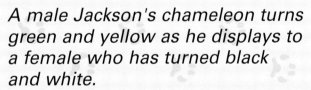

A male Jackson's chameleon turns green and yellow as he displays to a female who has turned black and white.

Chameleons often change colour to make themselves difficult to see. They may turn brown or grey on tree bark, or green among leaves. They also do it to show off. Males often 'fight' each other by displaying extra-bright colours, and the loser may actually turn white with fear!

Dazzling cuttlefish

It takes a chameleon several seconds to change colour, but a cuttlefish can do it in a split second. It uses the same system of variable colour dots, but they work much more quickly. A cuttlefish can make bands of colour ripple across its body in a dazzling light show, then switch them off instantly when it wants to hide. Many squids and octopuses, which are both related to cuttlefish, can do the same thing.

You cannot tell from the photo, but the stripes on this cuttlefish are moving across its body like ripples on a pond.

Ultimate camouflage

The animals with the best **camouflage** of all are **transparent**, meaning their enemies look right through them. Quite a lot of sea creatures are transparent. Many prawns and shrimps have almost see-through bodies, as do most of the tiny animals that live in the **plankton**. These small planktonic animals are eaten by bigger creatures such as jellyfish and comb jellies, and many of these are transparent too.

Comb jellies look a bit like plastic bags that have been filled with water. They get their name from the rows of small moving 'combs' on their bodies, which they use to drive themselves through the water. Their bodies are hard to see, but their rippling comb rows gleam with rainbow light that is reflected and scattered from special light-producing **organs** under the skin.

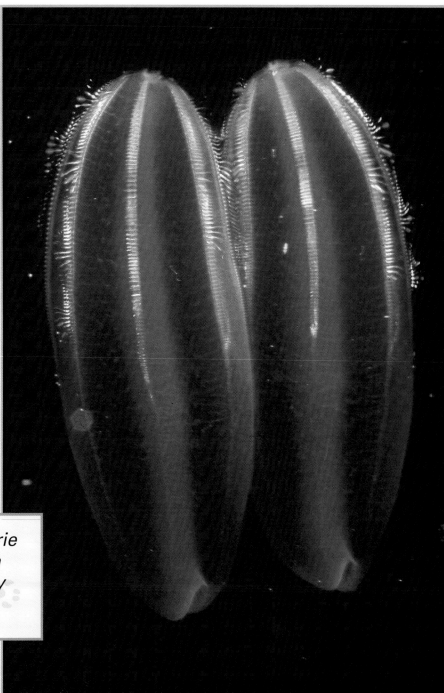

Two comb jellies glow with eerie light in the Arctic Ocean. When they are not lit up like this, they are almost invisible.

Strange, hollow, tube-shaped creatures called salps drift through the surface layers of the ocean, forming invisible groups that can be longer than a whale!

X-ray fish

The glass catfish that lives in rivers in south-eastern Asia is one of the few transparent animals that has a skeleton inside its body. All its bones are visible through its transparent body, just as if it were under an x-ray. You can also see all its organs. Yet the transparency provides excellent camouflage, which is just as well because the fish cannot swim very fast to escape its enemies.

Although you can see the eyes, bones and stomach of the glass catfish, its flesh is quite transparent.

Killers in the shade

Camouflage has its dangerous side. Many **predators** rely on good camouflage to make themselves invisible to their **prey**. The real masters of this are the **ambush** killers, that wait for victims to walk into their traps.

One of the most fearsome is the gaboon viper, a big African relative of the rattlesnakes, with huge poison **fangs**. Its massive body is patterned with diamonds and zigzags of colour. These can look quite dazzling, but among the dead leaves of the forest floor the pattern makes amazingly good camouflage, **disguising** the killer's snakey shape until it strikes with its deadly fangs.

The jagged lines and shapes on the gaboon viper's skin break up its outline, so it does not look like a snake at all.

Other snakes combine this sort of camouflage with a bit of cunning **mimicry**. The Australian death adder lurks in the shade, coiled head-to-tail and mostly hidden by its camouflage. The tip of its tail, however, is more brightly coloured, and the snake keeps twitching it to attract the attention of passing animals. They do not notice the snake's body, so the tail looks like a wriggling worm that might make a tasty snack. If an animal comes closer to investigate, the death adder suddenly lunges forward for the kill.

Many snakes that hunt in trees also depend on camouflage. The South American emerald tree boa is a beautiful green, which makes it almost invisible up among the leaves of the rainforest trees. The long-nosed tree snake has an unbelievably slender body so it looks like the thin stem of a climbing plant — until it moves.

Its tail looped tightly around a branch, an emerald tree boa waits for a victim to come within reach of its sharp teeth.

Underwater traps

Some of the most expertly **camouflaged** killers live under water. One of the weirdest is the matamata, a turtle that lives in the rivers of Amazonia, in South America. Its flattened shell looks like a rock, and it often has plants growing on it. Lying on the river bed, the turtle waits for small animals to swim by. When a victim is close enough, the turtle gapes its mouth wide open and sucks it in.

The American alligator snapping turtle has a similar hunting method. Its camouflage is almost as good, and it has a secret weapon. Its tongue is equipped with a **lure** that looks like a small, bright red worm. The turtle lies in the mud with its mouth open, wriggling its lure. Any fish that takes a close look is sure to get snapped up.

The red 'worm' on the tongue of this well-camouflaged alligator snapping turtle may be the last thing that a small fish ever sees.

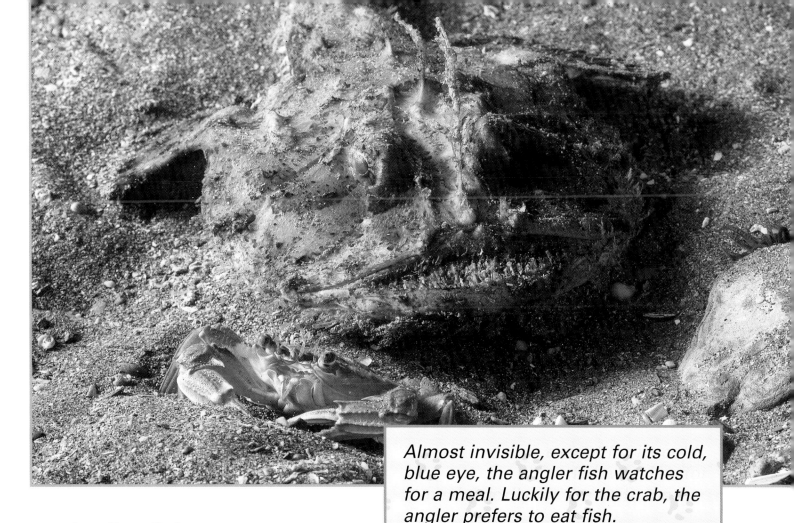

Almost invisible, except for its cold, blue eye, the angler fish watches for a meal. Luckily for the crab, the angler prefers to eat fish.

Angling fish

Fish use lures, too. The angler fish has a 'fishing rod' sticking out of its head that dangles a twitching lure in front of its huge mouth. Like the turtles it has excellent camouflage. Its seaweed-coloured body is fringed with small tassels of skin that hide its outline as it lies on the sea bed, and it often flicks sand on to its back to complete the effect.

Invisible, the angler waits for a small fish to swim within range. It tempts it closer by moving its lure, then suddenly opens its jaws to create a gaping hole. The water rushes in to fill the hole, taking the fish with it.

Some deepwater fish have lures that light up in the gloom of the deep ocean. These seem to attract other fish, and since the fish usually get eaten they don't get the chance to learn from their mistake.

Death in the flowers

Flowers can be deadly, or it seems that way. Sometimes, a butterfly looking for a drink of **nectar** lands on a flower and never leaves. Its dead body is still there an hour later, stuck to the petals. Or is it? Look closely, and you might see that a spider, coloured to be a perfect match with the flower petals, has **ambushed** the butterfly and killed it.

Known as crab or flower spiders, these ambush killers have strong front legs and a quick-acting poisonous bite (although they can't harm people). Each spider sits in a flower waiting for an insect to land, then grabs it and stabs it with its **fangs**. The poison works quickly, dissolving the insect's flesh inside its hard skin. The spider then sucks it dry, leaving just an empty shell.

Flowery mantids

One type of insect — the flower mantid — uses the same tactic. In some ways flower mantids are rather like flowery versions of leaf insects, because their bodies are shaped and coloured to look like flower petals. Some are creamy white, while others are a gorgeous rose pink. But to other insects they are deadly. A flower mantid climbs to the top of a plant stem and waits, looking just like a flower. If a bee or butterfly lands on it, the mantid seizes it in its strong front legs, which are toothed like the jaws of a trap, and eats it alive.

Coloured to look like an exotic orchid, this Malaysian flower mantid is a living trap for other insects that visit flowers for food.

Furry disguise

The animals that are our nearest relatives, **mammals**, do not generally have very clever **camouflage** compared to insects, **reptiles** or fish. Many mammals have brown or grey fur, and they are often paler underneath, to make their bodies look less solid.

Some mammals have more exciting camouflage. Many are hunters, like the various striped and spotted cats. The spots of a jaguar may look dazzling, but in the dappled shade of a **tropical** forest they **disguise** the hunter's outline and make it very hard to see. The stripes of a tiger do the same job, allowing it to creep very close to its **prey** before launching its attack.

The blotched, silver-grey coat of the central Asian snow leopard is a perfect match with the bare rock of its mountain home.

White as snow

In the far north, many mammals grow a thick coat of white fur to match the winter snow. They include the Arctic hare and Arctic fox, and the weasel and stoat. In spring their winter coats fall away to reveal thinner coats of brown or grey, which give better camouflage when the snow melts.

White fur gives the Arctic hare a good chance of not being seen in the winter snow, and escaping its enemies.

One Arctic animal that never loses its white coat is the polar bear. This is because it hunts seals out on the floating sea ice of the Arctic Ocean, in a world that is always white. In places where the ice melts in summer, polar bears simply stop hunting, and may not eat until the ice starts to form again.

Fact file

Most **camouflage** only fools animals that use their eyes to hunt for danger, such as most birds. It does not work at night, when animals depend on other senses, and it is not so effective against **mammals**, which depend more on their senses of hearing and smell. This may be why the animals with the best camouflage are creatures such as insects that are targeted by day-flying birds.

A few animals camouflage themselves with scent. Some butterfly caterpillars live in ants' nests, and eat the ants' young. They avoid being killed or thrown out because they smell of ants themselves. Some hunters also use scent to fool their **prey**. The **tropical** South and Central American bolas spider produces a scent like that of a female moth, and this attracts male moths into its trap.

Cryptic coloration works best for animals that spend the day sitting still. This explains why most moths have such good camouflage, even though they fly by night, when camouflage is useless. A moth perched on a tree trunk for the day would make an easy target for a bird if it was a bright colour. Many owls have good camouflage for the same reason.

In winter most Arctic foxes have white fur that hides them in the snow. However, in Iceland there is less snow than further north in the Arctic, and the local Arctic foxes stay brown all year. Natural selection has made the white variety disappear in Iceland.

Even plants may use camouflage. The strange 'living stone' plants of African deserts look almost exactly like pebbles, and this helps them avoid being eaten by desert animals desperate for a meal.

Many male birds have dazzling plumage of bright colours which helps them find mates and start families. This makes the risk of being seen by enemies worthwhile. The females, however, usually have good camouflage, so they are safer when they are sitting on their eggs and looking after their young.

The weirdest form of camouflage belongs to the hatchet fish that lives in the deep ocean. Its belly actually glows with light, which seems a strange way of hiding. But the glow matches the soft blue light that seeps down from the ocean surface, so the fish is invisible to killers attacking from below.

Glossary

ambush a trap set for a victim

breed come together to produce eggs or young

camouflage anything that hides an animal from its enemies or prey

cryptic coloration colours and patterns that match the animal's background

disguise feature that helps an animal pretend to be something else

fang hollow tooth that injects poison

frond leaf-like structure

industrial describes something connected with heavy industry such as steelworking or shipbuilding

lure bait that can be used again and again

mammal warm-blooded, furry animal that feeds its young on milk produced by the mother

midrib stiff central part of a leaf

mimicry pretending to be another animal, or plant

natural selection way some living things survive better than others, because they are better equipped for their way of life

nectar sweet, fragrant fluid produced by flowers, and drunk by insects and birds

organ part of an animal's body with a special use

plankton community of living things that drifts in the oceans

plumage pattern and form of a bird's feathers

predator animal that kills and eats other animals

prey animals that are killed and eaten by other animals

reptile scaly animal like a snake or a lizard

roost stop flying and settle down for the night, or day

sap fluid that carries sugar and other substances around plants

transparent describes something that allows light to shine right through it so that what is behind it can be seen

tropical describes hot regions of the world where the sun is directly overhead for part of the year

vein in plants, one of the small lines that spread out across leaves

Index

Titles in the *Amazing Nature* series include:

Hardback   0 431 18569 7

Hardback   0 431 18566 2

Hardback   0 431 18570 0

Hardback   0 431 18565 4

Hardback   0 431 18568 9

Hardback   0 431 18567 0

Find out about the other titles in this series on our website www.heinemann.co.uk/library